Spiralise your vegetables

Text, photographs and styling: Zoé Armbruster

MURDOCH BOOKS

SYDNEY · LONDON

Contents

Introduction

I am always on the lookout for creative ways to eat healthily, so the spiraliser immediately caught my attention. It means you can elegantly transform your vegetables into spaghetti, ribbons and tagliatelle. You can now eat pasta guilt free and enjoy a balanced meal with a flick of the wrist!

The fresh and innovative recipes in this book allow you to indulge yourself while maintaining a healthy glow and above all a healthy figure! With very few kilojoules, spiralised fruit and vegetables have lots of benefits for your system: they improve your digestion, give you more energy, bolster your immune system … and in general help you have a more nutritious diet that is still varied, original and delicious.

Fruits and vegetables are nutrient-rich foods and essential for keeping your body running smoothly. Thanks to this latest kitchen tool, it becomes very easy to eat them at each meal without even realising it. For parents with children who are fussy eaters, this is a good trick to put on the urgent list!

If you are not the happy owner of a spiraliser, you can use a mandoline with a julienne blade and slice the vegetable lengthways. If you don't have a mandoline, you can use a knife to slice vegetables into thin slivers, then recut into spaghetti.

With a vegetable peeler, you can make ribbons by peeling thin strips down the length of the vegetable; then you can turn them into tagliatelle by slicing them in two lengthways.

To make other recipes besides those based on zucchini (courgettes), cucumber, carrots and other long vegetables, I recommend you buy a more sophisticated model than the 'pencil sharpener' style (the price is about the same), with handles and suction pads.

Zoé Armbruster

Beetroot salad
with blood oranges

Serves 4 • Preparation time 20 mins • Cooking time 10 mins • Resting time 5 mins • Difficulty ★★ • Cost $
Equipment: Spiraliser

Ingredients

Red beetroot (beet) 1
Yellow beetroot (beets) 2
Olive oil
Blood oranges 2
Oranges 2
Lemon juice.....................................1 tablespoon
Lime juice.......................................1 tablespoon
Red onion...¼
Chervil ....A few leaves
Salt and pepper

Recipe

1. Preheat the oven to 180°C (350°F). Using the spiraliser, turn the beetroot into spaghetti. Dress the spaghetti with a drizzle of olive oil and season with salt. Bake in the oven for about 10 minutes.

2. Peel the blood oranges and slice one of them into rounds and the other into segments, removing the white membrane. Repeat with the regular oranges. Squeeze whatever is left of all the oranges into a bowl to extract the maximum amount of juice. Add the lemon and lime juice.

3. Place all the oranges on top of the beetroot. Slice the onion into very thin rings and sprinkle over the top.

4. Pour over the citrus juices, then another drizzle of olive oil. Season with salt and pepper. Set aside in the refrigerator for 5 minutes and scatter with chervil before serving.

Cucumber salad
with prawns and mango

Serves 4 • Preparation time 15 mins • Difficulty ★ • Cost $$
Equipment: Spiraliser

Ingredients

Telegraph (long) cucumbers 2
Red onion..½
Mango 1
Lemon...1
Cooked prawns (shrimp) 16
Olive oil
Dill...A few sprigs
Salt and pepper

Recipe

1. Spiralise the cucumbers and slice a few rounds from the left-over pieces. Slice the onion into very thin rings. Slice the mango around the stone, then lengthways into very thin slices. Zest and juice the lemon.

2. Combine the prawns, cucumber, onion and mango in a salad bowl, then dress with olive oil and lemon juice. Season with salt and pepper and sprinkle with dill and lemon zest.

Potato rosti
with smoked salmon

Makes 6 rosti • Preparation time 20 mins • Cooking time about 10 mins per rosti • Difficulty ★ • Cost $$
Equipment: Spiraliser

Ingredients

Medium-sized boiling (waxy) potatoes..............6
Red onion.................................1 small
Plain (all-purpose) flour................ 3 tablespoons
Egg 1
Vegetable oil (for pan-frying)
Smoked salmon...........................150 g (5½ oz)
Crème fraîche..................................6 teaspoons
Dill...A few sprigs
Salt and pepper

Recipe

1. Peel and spiralise the potatoes and onion. Combine the potatoes, onion, flour and beaten egg in a bowl. Season with salt and pepper.

2. Heat 3 tablespoons of vegetable oil in a frying pan and add a spoonful of the potato mixture. Flatten lightly with a spatula and let it brown for about 5 minutes on each side.

3. Transfer the rosti to some paper towels to drain then repeat the process, adding 1 tablespoon of oil each time.

4. Place a piece of smoked salmon and 1 teaspoon of crème fraîche on each rosti. Garnish with sprigs of dill, season with salt and pepper and serve.

Suggestion

These rosti are delicious with a rocket (arugula) salad.

Refreshing salad
with cucumber, soya beans and ginger sauce

Serves 4 • Preparation time 10 mins • Cooking time 10 mins • Difficulty ★ • Cost $
Equipment: Spiraliser

Ingredients

For the sauce

Olive oil .... 4 tablespoons
Sesame oil..................................... 2 tablespoons
Lemon juice.................................... 2 tablespoons
Soy sauce .... 2 teaspoons
Grated fresh ginger .... 1 teaspoon
Espelette pepper
Pepper

For the vegetable noodles

Spring onions (scallions) 2
Telegraph (long) cucumbers 2
Mint...A few leaves
Olive oil ....1 drizzle
Soya beans (fresh or frozen).........150 g (5½ oz)
Sesame seeds .... 3 tablespoons

Variation

You can replace the Espelette pepper with paprika.
You can replace the sesame seeds with gomasio
(toasted sesame salt).

Recipe

1. Mix together all of the sauce ingredients in a bowl.

2. Thinly slice the spring onions. Peel and spiralise the cucumbers. Finely chop the mint.

3. Heat the olive oil in a frying pan and lightly brown the soya beans.

4. Combine the cucumber, onion, soya beans and mint, then pour the sauce over and mix together well. Sprinkle with sesame seeds and serve.

Cabbage coleslaw
with granny smith apples

Serves 4 • Preparation time 10 mins • Difficulty ★ • Cost S
Equipment: Spiraliser

Ingredients

Granny smith apples...2
White cabbage...½
Red cabbage..½
Shelled pistachio nuts.........................30 g (1 oz)
Salt and pepper

For the sauce

Olive oil .... 2 tablespoons
Lemon juice....................................1 tablespoon
Honey...1 tablespoon
Chia seeds ....1 tablespoon

Recipe

1. Make the sauce by mixing together the olive oil, lemon juice, honey and chia seeds.

2. Spiralise the apples and finely shred the cabbage leaves to make a julienne.

3. Combine the cabbage, apples and pistachios in a salad bowl. Pour the sauce over and mix together well. Adjust the seasoning before serving.

Rice paper rolls
with shiitake, turnip and mango sauce

Makes 8 rolls • Preparation time 25 mins • Cooking time 5 mins • Difficulty ★ ★ ★ • Cost $$
Equipment: Spiraliser, food processor

Ingredients

Rice vermicelli ....60 g (2¼ oz)
Carrot 1
Turnips...2
Shiitake mushrooms ....70 g (2½ oz)
Rice paper wrappers 8
Bunch of mint..1
Bunch of Thai basil 1
Sesame seeds .... 2 tablespoons

For the sauce

Mango 1
Lime ....½
Mint leaves...5

Recipe

1. Place the vermicelli in a bowl and cover with salted boiling water, then let them rest for 5 minutes. Drain and set aside.

2. Peel the carrot, wash the turnips, then spiralise the carrot and turnips. Slice the mushrooms very thinly.

3. Soak the rice paper wrappers in a large bowl of cold water for about 10 seconds, one at a time, until they soften, then place them on a dry tea towel (dish towel).

4. Scatter a few leaves of mint and basil on the wrappers and place a large clump of noodles on each. Add three slivers of mushroom, a little turnip and carrot, and sprinkle with sesame seeds. Fold in the edges of each wrapper then roll up tightly to completely enclose the filling.

5. Make the sauce: peel and cut up the mango. Blend the mango, mint and the juice and zest of the half lime in a food processor.

6. Serve the rolls with a ramekin of sauce on the side.

Jar salad
to take away

Makes 1 jar • Preparation time 20 mins • Cooking time 15 mins • Difficulty ★ • Cost $
Equipment: Spiraliser, mason-style jar, food processor

Ingredients

Zucchini (courgette)..1
Quinoa...40 g (1½ oz)
Kale..A few leaves
Feta cheese ....30 g (1 oz)

For the sauce

Lime ....½
Avocado ....½
Coconut or almond milk.................. 2 tablespoons
Salt and pepper

Note

It is important to pour the sauce into the bottom of the jar first, then carefully arrange the salad ingredients on top, so the ingredients keep their freshness.

Recipe

1. Spiralise the zucchini. Rinse the quinoa. Pour the quinoa into a saucepan with a pinch of salt and almost twice its volume of water. Bring to the boil, lower the heat and cook, covered, on a low heat until the water is absorbed, about 15 minutes. Turn off the heat and let the quinoa swell up, covered, for another 10 minutes; this will make the quinoa fluffier.

2. Make the sauce: juice the half lime. Blend the avocado with the coconut or almond milk and the lime juice in a food processor, then season.

3. Remove the tough ribs of the kale leaves. Pour the sauce into the jar first. Gently lay the zucchini spaghetti on top, then the quinoa and kale leaves. Cut the feta into cubes and place it on top of the kale before closing the jar.

Flaked cod
with black radish tagliatelle and turmeric

Serves 4 • Preparation time 25 mins • Cooking time 30 mins • Difficulty ★ • Cost $$$
Equipment: Spiraliser, oven grill (broiler), steamer

Ingredients

White daikon radishes.......................................2
Garlic...2 cloves
French shallots...2
Olive oil .... 4 tablespoons
Ground turmeric .... 1 teaspoon
Coconut oil .... 4 tablespoons
Cod (or other firm white fish,
such as blue-eye)....................................4 fillets
Lemon juice................................... 4 tablespoons
Oregano...A few sprigs
Salt and pepper

Recipe

1. Spiralise the radishes, then steam for about 10 minutes.

2. Preheat the grill (broiler) to medium–high. Peel and chop the garlic and shallots, then mix them with the radish, olive oil and turmeric. Season with salt and pepper and place under the grill for 15 minutes.

3. Melt the coconut oil in a frying pan over medium–high heat, then add the cod fillets and brown for about 4 minutes on each side. Season with salt and pepper. Remove the fillets and add the lemon juice to the pan, heat for 1 minute, stirring with a wooden spatula to scrape up any bits from the base of the pan.

4. Flake the fillets and combine them with the radish, dress with the lemon–coconut oil sauce and scatter with a few sprigs of oregano.

Beetroot risotto

Serves 4 • Preparation time 20 mins • Cooking time 30 mins • Difficulty ★ • Cost $
Equipment: Spiraliser

Ingredients

Beetroot (beets) 2
Red onion...1
Melted butter .... 4 tablespoons
Olive oil .... 4 tablespoons
Arborio or other risotto rice............350 g (12 oz)
Dry white wine .... 250 ml (9 fl oz/1 cup)
Stock...........................1.5 litres (52 fl oz/6 cups)
Grated parmesan cheese.................80 g (2¾ oz)

Recipe

1. Peel and spiralise the beetroot; finely chop the onion.

2. Heat the butter and olive oil in a deep frying pan over medium–high heat. Add the onion and lightly brown it for about 6 minutes. Add the rice and cook it, stirring, for 2 minutes, until translucent.

3. Add the beetroot spaghetti to the frying pan, mix again and cook for 1 minute. Next, add the wine and, once it has been absorbed by the rice, add a ladleful of stock. Stir again. Once the stock has been completely absorbed, repeat this process until all of the stock has been used up (about 20 minutes cooking time).

4. Sprinkle with parmesan, wait for 2 minutes, then mix vigorously and serve.

Chicken skewers
on a bed of carrots with peanut and ginger sauce

Serves 4 • Preparation time 25 mins • Marinating time 1 hr • Cooking time 20 mins • Difficulty ★ • Cost $$
Equipment: Spiraliser, wooden skewers, oven grill (broiler), food processor, plastic wrap, steamer

Ingredients

Skinless chicken breast fillets .... 900 g (2 lb)
Garlic cloves 2
Fresh ginger ....50 g (1¾ oz)
Coconut milk ....300 ml (10½ fl oz)
Ground turmeric .... 1 teaspoon
Peanut or almond butter .... 3 tablespoons
Carrots (white or orange)...............................10
Toasted peanuts...........................100 g (3½ oz)

Recipe

1. Cut the chicken breast fillets into regular 3 cm (1¼ inch) cubes and place them in a shallow bowl. Peel and chop the garlic. Peel and grate the ginger. Mix these two ingredients with the coconut milk, turmeric and peanut or almond butter. Pour the mixture over the chicken, cover with plastic wrap and marinate for 1 hour in the refrigerator.

2. Preheat the oven grill (broiler) to medium–high. Drain the chicken and thread the pieces onto wooden skewers. Place under the grill and grill (broil) for 10 minutes, turning regularly.

3. Spiralise the carrots and steam them for about 10 minutes.

4. Heat the marinade in a small saucepan over medium heat, then blend it in a food processor into a smooth sauce (add a little water if necessary).

5. Serve the skewers on a bed of carrots with the sauce and the peanuts, roughly chopped.

Carbonara
with asparagus and zucchini

Serves 4 • Preparation time 15 mins • Cooking time 15 mins • Difficulty ★ • Cost $
Equipment: Spiraliser

Ingredients

Zucchini (courgettes)......................................10
Green asparagus .... 500 g (1 lb 2 oz/1 bunch)
Smoked bacon................................ 6 thin slices
Eggs...2
Egg yolks 2
Parmesan cheese..........................100 g (3½ oz)
Olive oil
Salt and pepper

Recipe

1. Spiralise the zucchini. Cut the asparagus spears into long pieces. Chop the smoked bacon and brown it in a frying pan with a little olive oil over medium-high heat. Remove the bacon from the pan and put it in a mixing bowl. Grind a little pepper into the oil left in the pan, then add the asparagus and a pinch of salt. Cook for about 5 minutes, until the asparagus is tender.

2. Meanwhile, break the eggs over the bacon, add the egg yolks and parmesan, and mix together well. Add the asparagus and stir continuously for 15 seconds to melt the cheese.

3. Heat a little oil in the pan again and cook the zucchini with 3 tablespoons of water for 5 to 7 minutes.

4. Add the zucchini and everything else in the pan to the mixing bowl. Mix again and serve immediately.

Ramen
with winter radish

Serves 4 • Preparation time 25 mins • Cooking time 25 mins • Difficulty ★ ★ • Cost $$
Equipment: Spiraliser, 4 deep bowls

Ingredients

Eggs 2
Winter radish (purple or white) .... 1 small
Spring onions (scallions) 4
Lime .... ½
Sesame oil .... 1 tablespoon
Freshly grated ginger .... 2 teaspoons
English spinach .... 450 g (1 lb)
Baby shiitake mushrooms .... 170 g (6 oz)
Snow peas (mangetout) .... 150 g (5½ oz)
Stock .... 1.5 litres (52 fl oz/6 cups)
Soy sauce .... 1 tablespoon
Rice vinegar .... 1 tablespoon
Salt and pepper

Recipe

1. Place the eggs in a saucepan filled with water over medium-high heat, bring to the boil, then remove the pan from the heat. Leave the eggs in the hot water for 10 minutes before rinsing them under cold water, shelling them and cutting them in half. Set the eggs aside.

2. Spiralise the radish and thinly slice the spring onions. Juice the half lime. Heat the sesame oil in a fairly wide frying pan over medium-high heat, add the ginger and half the spring onions and cook for 1 minute. Add the spinach, mushrooms and snow peas, then season. Add the stock and, when it comes to the boil, add the radish spaghetti, soy sauce, rice vinegar and lime juice, and simmer for 5 minutes.

3. Serve the soup in bowls, adding a halved egg to each. Sprinkle over the rest of the spring onions.

Carrot farinata
with yoghurt sauce

Serves 6 • Preparation time 20 mins • Cooking time 10 mins • Difficulty ★★ • Cost $$
Equipment: Spiraliser

Ingredients

For the batter

Chickpea flour (besan)... 150 g (5½ oz/1¼ cups)
Almond milk..........................230 ml (7¾ fl oz)
Olive oil .... 2 tablespoons
Carrots 2
Coconut oil
(or other oil, for pan-frying) .... 1 teaspoon
Salt and pepper

For the sauce

Cornichons.......................................8
Green chilli.......................................1
Flat-leaf (Italian) parsley ....A few sprigs
Dill...A few sprigs
Lemon...½
Greek-style yoghurt...................... 4 tablespoons
Worcestershire sauce......................... ½ teaspoon
Chilli sauce (Tabasco-style).......................A dash
Salt and pepper

To serve

Seed sprouts... A few
Salad leaves .... A few

Recipe

1. Make the batter: mix together the chickpea flour and a generous pinch of salt and pepper in a large mixing bowl. Mix in the almond milk and olive oil and let the batter rest, covered with a tea towel (dish towel).

2. Make the sauce: chop the cornichons, chilli and herbs. Zest the half lemon. Mix together the cornichons, chilli, parsley, dill and zest in a small bowl with the Greek-style yoghurt, Worcestershire sauce and chilli sauce. Mix together well and season.

3. Spiralise the carrots and add them to the batter; mix together well. Melt the coconut oil in a frying pan over medium–high heat. Pour in the batter and let it cook for about 5 minutes. When the farinata is golden around the edges, turn it over (with the help of a plate if it is a bit fragile) and cook for another 5 minutes on the other side.

4. Serve each portion with a spoonful of sauce, seed sprouts and salad leaves.

Courgetti alle vongole

Serves 4 • Preparation time 20 mins • Cooking time 10 mins • Difficulty ★ • Cost $$
Equipment: Spiraliser, steamer

Ingredients

Clams (vongole) .... 1 kg (2 lb 4 oz)
Bunch of flat-leaf (Italian) parsley .... 1 small
Garlic .... 4 cloves
Zucchini (courgettes) 10
Olive oil .... 4 tablespoons
Dry white wine .... 250 ml (9 fl oz/1 cup)
Espelette pepper .... 1 tablespoon
Salt and pepper

Variation

You can replace the Espelette pepper with paprika.

Recipe

1. Rinse the clams carefully under cold water and throw away any shells that are already open. Chop the parsley (set some aside for serving) and peel and chop the garlic. Spiralise the zucchini and steam it for 5 minutes.

2. Heat the olive oil in a frying pan over medium heat. Add the garlic and parsley and gently sauté for a few minutes. Season with salt and pepper. Add the clams, white wine and Espelette pepper. Mix together well, cover and cook for 5 minutes. When the clams open, they are ready. Discard any that stay closed.

3. Mix together the zucchini spaghetti and clams, then scatter with a little chopped parsley. Mix again and serve.

Spiral tart
with zucchini and carrot

Serves 8 • Preparation time 45 mins • Pastry resting time 1 hour • Cooking time 40 mins • Difficulty ★ ★ ★ • Cost S
Equipment: Spiraliser (tagliatelle blade), food processor (optional), 28 cm (11¼ in) flan (tart) tin, rolling pin, plastic wrap, baking paper

Ingredients

For the pastry

Softened butter ....150 g (5½ oz)
Plain (all-purpose) flour......250 g (9 oz/1⅓ cups)
Egg 1
Breadmaker seed mix.................... 2 tablespoons
Grated parmesan cheese....................25 g (1 oz)
Olive oil ....A drizzle
Pepper

For the filling

Carrots 6
Zucchini (courgettes, yellow and green).............6
Thin (pouring) cream...............130 ml (4½ fl oz)
Egg 1
Salt and pepper

Recipe

1. Make the pastry: cream the softened butter in a mixing bowl or the bowl of a food processor. Add the flour, egg, seed mix, parmesan and season with pepper. Add 6 tablespoons of water and work the ingredients together. Once the dough is smooth, shape it into a ball, wrap in plastic wrap and place in the refrigerator for 1 hour.

2. Preheat the oven to 210°C (410°F). Roll the pastry out to a thickness of about 5 mm (¼ inch) on a floured work surface. Butter and flour a flan (tart) tin and line with the pastry. Prick the pastry base with a fork. Place a circle of baking paper over the base and fill with baking beads to stop the pasta from puffing up. Bake for about 10 minutes.

3. Make the filling: slice the carrots and zucchini into ribbons with the tagliatelle blade (or a peeler). Place the ribbons on top of each other, then cut them into semi-circles of equal size. Pour 70 ml (2¼ fl oz) of the cream over the pre-cooked tart base, season with salt and pepper, then arrange the vegetables, starting from the edge and alternating carrots and green and yellow zucchini until you reach the middle of the tart. Mix the remaining cream with the egg and season with salt and pepper. Pour this mixture over the tart and bake for 30 minutes until the tart is golden brown.

4. Drizzle with a little olive oil and serve.

Cucumber ribbons
with tuna and avocado-pepita pesto

Serves 4 • Preparation time 10 mins • Difficulty ★ • Cost $$
Equipment: Spiraliser (tagliatelle blade), food processor

Ingredients

Avocado 1
Lemon....................................1 small
Basil................................20 g (¾ oz)
Pepitas (pumpkin seeds) ....30 g (1 oz)
Olive oil ....3 tablespoons
Telegraph (long) cucumber.............................1
Tuna fillet (sashimi grade) ....650 g (1 lb 7 oz)
Salt and pepper

Recipe

1. Cut open the avocado and scoop out the flesh. Squeeze the lemon. Place the avocado, basil, pepitas and lemon juice in the bowl of a food processor and blend them together. Add the olive oil and about 2 tablespoons of water to loosen the sauce. Season with salt and pepper.

2. Slice the cucumber into ribbons with the tagliatelle blade. Cut the tuna into small 2 cm (¾ inch) cubes.

3. Serve the cucumber ribbons with the tuna and the avocado-pepita pesto.

Turbot fillets
with mustard, parsnip tagliatelle and toasted almonds

Serves 4 • Preparation time 40 mins • Cooking time 40 mins • Difficulty ★★★ • Cost $$$
Equipment: Spiraliser (tagliatelle blade), foil, steamer

Ingredients

French shallots...2 small
Turbot (or other flaky white fish, such as
    John Dory) ......4 fillets, 120 g (4¼ oz) each
    Dry white wine ....100 ml (3½ fl oz)
    Fish stock...................200 ml (7 fl oz)
    Softened butter...........100 g (3½ oz)
    Wholegrain mustard.... 3 tablespoons
    Parsnips..................1 kg (2 lb 4 oz)
    Cherry tomatoes ....100 g (3½ oz)
    Chopped flat-leaf (Italian)
    parsley ....2 tablespoons
A few toasted flaked almonds
Salt and pepper

Recipe

1. Preheat the oven to 180°C (350°F). Finely chop the shallots and arrange them in a buttered flameproof oven dish. Lay the turbot fillets on top and pour in the white wine and fish stock. Season.

2. Cover the dish with buttered foil and bring to the boil on the stove before transferring to the oven for 10 minutes. Remove the fillets and keep warm.

3. Reduce the sauce and add the butter, little by little, then the mustard.

4. Peel and slice the parsnips into tagliatelle then steam them for 10 minutes.

5. Assemble each serving by placing a fillet of fish on a bed of parsnip, divide the sauce between the plates and garnish with halved cherry tomatoes, parsley and toasted almonds.

Turkey burgers
with Moroccan spices and avocado aïoli

Makes 4 large or 6 small burgers • Preparation time 20 mins • Resting time 15 mins • Cooking time 10 mins
Difficulty ★★★ • Cost $$ - $$$
Equipment: Spiraliser

Ingredients

For the hamburgers

Large zucchini (courgette).................................1
Minced (ground) turkey............500 g (1 lb 2 oz)
Spring onions (scallions) 4
Garlic..1 clove
Finely chopped mint.......................2 tablespoons
Finely chopped parsley ....2 tablespoons
Sriracha sauce
(or other chilli sauce).......................1 tablespoon
Ground cumin.................................... 1 teaspoon
Whole egg, beaten...1
Salt and pepper
Olive oil (for cooking the burgers)

For the aïoli

Avocado 1
Greek-style yoghurt......................2 tablespoons
Garlic...2 cloves
Lime 1
Sriracha sauce
(or other chilli sauce).......................1 tablespoon
Horseradish cream............................1 tablespoon

To serve

Baby salad leaves...................................... A few
Burger buns ....4 large or 6 small

Recipe

1. Spiralise the zucchini into spaghetti. Mix together all of the hamburger ingredients except the olive oil in a mixing bowl. Divide the mixture into four or six patties depending on what size you want. Rest them in the refrigerator for about 15 minutes.

2. Heat some olive oil in a frying pan, over medium–high heat. Add the hamburger patties and cook them for about 5 minutes on each side.

3. Meanwhile, make the aïoli: purée the avocado. Place it in a bowl and mix it well with the rest of the ingredients. Adjust the seasoning.

4. Serve in the buns, with a few baby salad leaves and the aïoli.

Tip

These burgers are delicious served with
sweet potato spiral fries.

Carrot pasta
with sage, pumpkin and pancetta

Serves 4 • Preparation time 20 mins • Cooking time 20 mins • Difficulty ★★ • Cost $$
Equipment: Spiraliser, steamer

Ingredients

Carrots .... 6 large
Garlic .... 2 cloves
French shallot 1
Sage .... 5 leaves
Pancetta .... 250 g (9 oz)
Espelette pepper .... 1 teaspoon
Pumpkin purée
(tinned or frozen) .... 300 g (10½ oz)
Thickened (whipping) cream
(30% fat) .... 300 ml (10½ fl oz)
Ground nutmeg .... 1 pinch
Salt and pepper

Variation

You can replace the Espelette pepper with paprika.

Recipe

1. Peel and spiralise the carrots into spaghetti. Steam them for 8 minutes.

2. Peel and chop the garlic, and chop the shallot and sage. Sauté the pancetta in a dry frying pan for 5 to 7 minutes over medium–high heat until it is nice and crispy. Remove with a slotted spoon and set aside.

3. Add the sage, shallot and garlic to the pan with the Espelette pepper and stir well, making sure not to burn the garlic, for about 30 seconds (if the frying pan is too hot, take it off the heat and wait a little bit). Add the pumpkin purée and let it simmer on low heat for 2 to 3 minutes, then add the cream and nutmeg. Adjust the seasoning. Rest in the frying pan for 5 minutes.

4. Serve the carrot spaghetti with the still-warm sauce.

Beef bibimbap

Serves 4 • Preparation time 35 mins • Marinating time 15 mins • Cooking time 20 mins • Difficulty ★★★ • Cost $$$
Equipment: Spiraliser, 4 deep bowls

Ingredients

For the pickled vegetables

Carrots 4
Telegraph (long) cucumber..............................1
Rice vinegar .... 4 tablespoons
Sugar...15 g (½ oz)
Salt.. 1 large pinch

For the rice

Sushi rice ....350 g (12 oz)
Salt.. 1 teaspoon

For the spinach

Baby English spinach ....350 g (12 oz)
Sesame oil.. 2 teaspoons
Sesame seeds .... 2 teaspoons
Salt

For the beef

Rump steak (or sirloin or fillet) ......350 g (12 oz)
Soy sauce.................................... 3 tablespoons
Maple syrup .... 2 tablespoons
Sesame oil.................................... 2 tablespoons
Sriracha sauce (or other chilli sauce) .. 1 teaspoon
Garlic .... 1 clove

For the topping

Eggs...4
Sriracha sauce (or other hot chilli sauce)
Olive oil
Salt and pepper

Recipe

1. Spiralise the carrots and cucumber, then marinate them in the rice vinegar, sugar and salt for 15 minutes. Drain.

2. Rinse the rice, then place it in a saucepan with 500 ml (17 fl oz) of water and some salt. Bring to the boil then cook over low heat for 12 to 15 minutes, until the liquid has been absorbed. Stir the rice and let it rest, covered, for 5 minutes.

3. Blanch the spinach. Plunge it into iced water after blanching, then squeeze out the liquid. Mix the sesame oil, sesame seeds and a pinch of salt with the spinach.

4. Slice the beef very thinly and mix all of the marinade ingredients together with 3 tablespoons of water in a bowl. Marinate the beef for a few minutes, then drain. Set the marinade aside. In three batches, brown the meat on each side in a large frying pan over medium-high heat. Set the meat aside. Add the marinade to the pan and bring to the boil. Add the beef. Let it simmer for 3 minutes and coat with the sauce. Take off the heat.

5. Heat a little olive oil in another frying pan and break in the eggs. Cook over low heat, on one side only, for about 3 minutes or until the white is cooked. Season with salt and pepper.

6. Divide the rice between the bowls. Add the meat, carrots and pickled cucumbers to the rice. Place an egg on top and sprinkle with sesame seeds; serve with a little sriracha sauce.

Pad Thai
with raw vegetables

Serves 4 • Preparation time 15 mins • Difficulty ★ • Cost $$

Ingredients

Carrots (red and/or orange) 4
White daikon radishes.......................................3
Radishes..10
Red cabbage...1
Spring onions (scallions) 4
Mint, basil and/or
coriander (cilantro).........................A few leaves
Bean sprouts ....200 g (7 oz)
Sesame seeds ....2 tablespoons
Tofu ....400 g (14 oz)

For the sauce

Limes 3
Peanut butter ....60 g (2¼ oz)
Soy sauce.....................................2 tablespoons
Honey...2 tablespoons
Grated fresh ginger ....2 teaspoons
Espelette pepper.............................. 1 teaspoon

Variation

You can replace the Espelette pepper with paprika.
You can replace the sesame seeds with gomasio
(toasted sesame salt).

Recipe

1. Peel and spiralise the carrots. Slice the radishes and cabbage very thinly. Finely chop the spring onions (white and green parts). Chop the herbs. Combine these ingredients in a large bowl with the bean sprouts and sesame seeds.

2. Prepare the tofu: press the excess moisture from the tofu using paper towels, then crumble it and add to the salad.

3. Make the sauce: juice the limes and mix together all of the sauce ingredients with 3 tablespoons of water until creamy. Pour the sauce over the salad just before serving.

Wild rice
with butternut pumpkin, pomegranate and pistachios

Serves 4 • Preparation time 20 mins • Cooking time about 1 hour • Difficulty ★ • Cost $$
Equipment: Spiraliser, food processor, baking tray, baking paper

Ingredients

Black rice ....200 g (7 oz)
Wild rice..200 g (7 oz)
Butternut pumpkin (squash, the less fibrous,
seedless part) ....½
Olive oil ....120 ml (4 fl oz)
Spring onions (scallions) 4
Pomegranate..1
Shelled pistachio nuts......................50 g (1¾ oz)
Red wine vinegar...........................3 tablespoons
Honey ....2 tablespoons
Salt and pepper

Recipe

1. Preheat the oven to 230°C (450°F). Cook the rices in a large saucepan of boiling water with a pinch of salt according to the packet instructions (about 35 to 40 minutes). Drain and rinse the rice to remove all the water and spread it out on a baking tray or plate to cool.

2. Meanwhile, peel and spiralise the pumpkin. Spread the pumpkin spaghetti over a baking tray covered with baking paper, pour over 3 tablespoons of the olive oil, season and bake for about 20 minutes. Let it cool.

3. Slice the spring onions on the diagonal (white and green parts). Remove the seeds from the pomegranate. Roughly chop the pistachios.

4. Blend together the red wine vinegar, honey and the remaining olive oil in a large bowl. Add the black and wild rice, the pumpkin spaghetti, spring onion, pomegranate seeds and pistachios. Adjust the seasoning and mix together.

Courgetti
with basil and walnut pesto

Serves 4 • Preparation time 15 mins • Cooking time 10 mins • Difficulty ★ • Cost $
Equipment: Spiraliser, food processor, steamer

Ingredients

Zucchini (courgettes)..8

For the pesto
Basil...40 g (1½ oz)
Walnuts............80 g (2¾ oz) + a few for garnish
Garlic...3 cloves
Olive oil ....100 ml (3½ fl oz)
Grated parmesan cheese.................50 g (1¾ oz)
Salt and pepper

Recipe

1. Spiralise the zucchini into spaghetti and steam for about 10 minutes.

2. Make the pesto: peel the garlic. Place the garlic, basil and walnuts into the bowl of a food processor. Season with salt and pepper, process everything together then add the olive oil and parmesan until you have a creamy sauce.

3. Serve the zucchini spaghetti with the pesto and a few roughly chopped walnuts.

Suggestion

If there is any pesto left over, crush and rub a little garlic on toast and spread it with pesto. It will be a delicious accompaniment for this dish.

Rice pudding
with pear and lavender

Serves 4 • Preparation time 10 mins • Cooking time 25 mins • Difficulty ★★★ • Cost $
Equipment: Spiraliser, 4 small ramekins

Ingredients

Milk .... 1 litre (35 fl oz/4 cups)
Sugar ....55 g (2 oz)
Vanilla bean 1
Lavender... 1 teaspoon
Short-grain rice ....130 g (4¾ oz)
Pear...1
Chopped roasted hazelnuts .... A few

Recipe

1. Heat the milk in a saucepan over medium heat with the sugar and the vanilla bean, split and scraped out. When the milk just comes to a bare simmer, add the lavender and pour in the rice. Cook for 25 minutes on a low heat, stirring regularly to prevent a skin forming on top.

2. Once the rice is cooked, remove the vanilla bean. Spiralise the pear.

3. Serve the rice pudding in ramekins. Top with the spiralised pear and sprinkle with hazelnuts.

Truffles
with cocoa and plantain

Makes 10 truffles • Preparation time 15 mins • Cooking time 3 mins • Chilling time 20 mins • Difficulty ★ • Cost $$
Equipment: Spiraliser, food processor

Ingredients

Plantains 2
Coconut oil (or other oil) ....1 tablespoon
Dates 8
Cocoa nibs.................................... 2 tablespoons
Unsweetened (Dutch) cocoa powder... 2 tablespoons
Desiccated coconut......................... 2 tablespoons
+ a little to serve

Recipe

1. Trim the ends of the plantains so they are straight. Use the tip of a knife to split the skin down the length of the plantains and peel it off. Spiralise the plantains.

2. Heat the coconut oil in a small frying pan over medium-high heat. Add the plantain spirals and sauté for about 3 minutes, then remove from the heat.

3. Pit the dates and blend them to a paste in a food processor. If they don't become smooth, add 1 teaspoon of water and blend again; repeat this process until you have a smooth paste.

4. Add the plantain, cocoa nibs, cocoa and desiccated coconut to the bowl of the food processor and keep blending until the mixture is sticky and homogeneous.

5. Transfer the mixture to a bowl and shape 10 small truffles in the palms of your hands. Roll in a little desiccated coconut if you like, place carefully on a plate and refrigerate for about 20 minutes.

Sweet potato waffles
with berries

Serves 4 • Preparation time 10 mins • Cooking time 5 mins per waffle • Difficulty ★ • Cost $$
Equipment: Spiraliser, waffle maker

Ingredients

Sweet potatoes 2
Ground cinnamon .... 1 teaspoon
Eggs, beaten...2
Vanilla extract .... 1 teaspoon
Blueberries.................................150 g (5½ oz)
Maple syrup .... 1 tablespoon per waffle
Raspberries ....150 g (5½ oz)
Flaked almonds .... A few
Olive oil, coconut oil or other oil
(for cooking the waffles)

Suggestion

The waffles must be served with maple syrup,
or they won't have any sweetness.

Recipe

1. Heat the waffle maker. Peel and spiralise the sweet potatoes.

2. Combine the sweet potato spirals with the ground cinnamon in a bowl. Heat a little oil in a frying pan over medium-high heat. Add the sweet potatoes, cover and let them cook for about 6 minutes, until tender; add 1 tablespoon of water if necessary.

3. Transfer to a mixing bowl and add the beaten eggs, vanilla extract and blueberries (reserve some to serve). Make sure the spirals are saturated with the mixture.

4. Grease the waffle maker and carefully pour in a quarter of the batter, making sure to fill the hollows. Let it cook for about 5 minutes, then repeat the process.

5. Serve with maple syrup, a few raspberries, blueberries and flaked almonds.

Gluten-free muffins
with chocolate and zucchini

Makes 12 muffins • Preparation time 10 mins • Cooking time 20 to 25 mins • Difficulty ★ • Cost $$
Equipment: Spiraliser, muffin tin

Ingredients

Zucchini (courgettes).............................2 small
Coconut oil ....110 g (3¾ oz)
Buckwheat flour ....100 g (3½ oz)
Coconut flour...............................60 g (2¼ oz)
Unsweetened (Dutch) cocoa powder....40 g (1½ oz)
Bicarbonate of soda (baking soda) ..... 1 teaspoon
Salt ....1 pinch
Honey......................................110 g (3¾ oz)
Vanilla extract ....2 teaspoons
Thickened (whipping) cream
(30% fat)....................................180 ml (6 fl oz)
Eggs, beaten...2
Chocolate chips...........................110 g (3¾ oz)
Puffed buckwheat........................... A few grains
Oil for the tin

Recipe

1. Preheat the oven to 180°C (350°F). Spiralise the zucchini, spread it out on paper towels and let the towels absorb the moisture for about 10 minutes.

2. Meanwhile, oil the muffin tin holes with a little coconut oil. Mix together the buckwheat flour, coconut flour, cocoa powder, bicarbonate of soda and salt.

3. Pour the honey, remaining coconut oil, vanilla extract and cream into a small bowl, add the beaten eggs and the zucchini and mix together well. Pour this wet mixture over the dry mixture and mix together to a smooth batter. Add the chocolate chips.

4. Pour the batter into the muffin holes and bake for 20 to 25 minutes. Insert the tip of a knife into a muffin to check whether it is done, the muffins are cooked when the knife comes out clean.

5. Sprinkle with a few grains of puffed buckwheat and eat them right away!

Yoghurt pots
with chestnut purée and apple

Serves 4 • Preparation time 5 mins • Difficulty: ★ • Cost $
Equipment: Spiraliser, 4 small ramekins

Ingredients

Fresh, unsalted ricotta cheese........230 g (8½ oz)
Greek-style yoghurt...................... 3 tablespoons
Honey... 2 tablespoons
Vanilla extract .... 1 teaspoon
Apple ....1 large
Crème de marrons
(chestnut purée).......................... 4 tablespoons
Meringue .... 1 small (about 60 g/2¼ oz)

Recipe

1. Gently combine the ricotta, yoghurt, honey and vanilla extract. Spiralise the apple.

2. Place 1 tablespoon of the crème de marrons in the bottom of each ramekin, then a little ricotta mixture and a few apple spirals on top.

3. Crumble the meringue and sprinkle some on top of each ramekin just before serving.

Mini fondant cakes
with chocolate and sweet potato

Makes 6 rosti • Preparation time 10 mins • Cooking time 25 mins • Resting time 5 mins • Difficulty ★ • Cost $
Equipment: Spiraliser, muffin tin

Ingredients

Sweet potato 1
Ground cinnamon .... 1 teaspoon
Bicarbonate of soda (baking soda) ..... 1 teaspoon
Desiccated coconut .... 2 tablespoons
Salt .... 1 pinch
Egg 1
Egg white 1
Honey .... 2 tablespoons
Vanilla extract .... 1 teaspoon
Chocolate chips .... 70 g (2½ oz)
Coconut oil or other oil

Suggestion

These little cakes are very moist because they don't contain
any flour. To stop the bottom from becoming soggy,
let them rest for 30 minutes before serving.

Recipe

1. Preheat the oven to 190°C (375°F). Oil the muffin tin holes and spiralise the sweet potato.

2. Mix together the sweet potato, cinnamon, bicarbonate of soda, coconut and salt in a bowl. Add the egg and egg white, the honey, vanilla extract and chocolate chips; mix together well.

3. Pour the mixture into the muffin tin holes, filling them up halfway. Bake for 20 to 25 minutes until they are firm on top. Insert the tip of a knife into a muffin to check whether it is done, the muffins should be moist in the middle. Let them rest for 5 minutes before removing from the tin.

Ice blocks
with elderberry and pear

Makes 6 ice blocks • Preparation time 5 mins • Freezing time 1 hour + 1 night • Difficulty ★ • Cost $

Equipment: Spiraliser, 6 ice block moulds and sticks

Ingredients

Pear...1
Elderberry syrup.....................100 ml (3½ fl oz)

Recipe

1. Spiralise the pear.

2. Mix the elderberry syrup with 500 ml (17 fl oz/ 2 cups) of water in a bowl; add the spiralised pear.

3. Pour into the moulds and place in the freezer for 1 hour. Add the ice block sticks and put back in the freezer to freeze overnight.

Measures and equivalents

Guide for measuring ingredients without a scale

Ingredients	1 teaspoon	1 tablespoon	1 cup
Butter	7 g (⅕ oz)	20 g (¾ oz)	–
Unsweetened (Dutch) cocoa powder	5 g (⅛ oz)	10 g (¼ oz)	90 g (3¼ oz)
Thickened (whipping cream), crème fraîche (30% fat)	15 ml (½ fl oz)	40 ml (1¼ fl oz)	250 ml (9 fl oz/ 1 cup)
Thin (pouring) cream	7 ml (¼ fl oz)	20 ml (½ fl oz)	250 ml (9 fl oz/ 1 cup)
Flour	3 g (⅒ oz)	10 g (¼ oz)	150 g (5½ oz)
Grated gruyère cheese	4 g (⅒ oz)	12 g (⅖ oz)	65 g (2½ oz)
Various liquids			
(water, oil, vinegar, alcohols)	5 ml (¼ fl oz)	20 ml (½ fl oz)	250 ml (9 fl oz/ 1 cup)
Cornflour (cornstarch)	3 g (⅒ oz)	10 g (¼ oz)	125 g (4½ oz)
Almond meal	6 g (⅕ oz)	15 g (½ oz)	100 g (3½ oz)
Raisins	8 g (³⁄₁₀ oz)	30 g (1 oz)	170 g (6 oz)
Rice	7 g (⅕ oz)	20 g (¾ oz)	200 g (7 oz)
Salt flakes	5 g (⅛ oz)	15 g (½ oz)	130 g (4¾ oz)
Couscous	5 g (⅛ oz)	15 g (½ oz)	190 g (6¾ oz)
Caster (superfine) sugar	5 g (⅛ oz)	15 g (½ oz)	220 g (7¾ oz)
Icing (confectioners') sugar	3 g (⅒ oz)	10 g (¼ oz)	125 g (4½ oz)

Guide to liquid measurements

1 liqueur glass = 30 ml (1 fl oz)
1 coffee cup = 80 to 100 ml (2½–3½ fl oz)
1 glass = 200 ml (7 fl oz)
1 mug = 300 ml (10½ fl oz)
1 bowl = 350 ml (12 fl oz)

Good to know

1 egg = 50 g (1¾ oz)
1 small knob of butter = 5 g (⅛ oz)
1 knob of butter = 15 to 20 g (½ to ¾ oz)

Regulating your oven

Temperature (°C)	(°F)
30	85
60	140
90	195
120	235
150	300
180	350
210	410
240	475
270	520

Published in 2017 by Murdoch Books, an imprint of Allen & Unwin
First published by Hachette Livre (Hachette Pratique) in 2016

Murdoch Books Australia
83 Alexander Street
Crows Nest NSW 2065
Phone: +61 (0) 2 8425 0100
Fax: +61 (0) 2 9906 2218
murdochbooks.com.au
info@murdochbooks.com.au

Murdoch Books UK
Ormond House
26–27 Boswell Street
London WC1N 3JZ
Phone: +44 (0) 20 8785 5995
murdochbooks.co.uk
info@murdochbooks.co.uk

For Corporate Orders & Custom Publishing contact our business development team at
salesenquiries@murdochbooks.com.au.

Publisher: Corinne Roberts
Translator: Melissa McMahon
Art Director: Antoine Béon
Graphic design of cover and internals: Studio-Allez
Production Manager: Rachel Walsh

A cataloguing-in-publication entry is available from the catalogue of the National Library of Australia at nla.gov.au.

ISBN 978 1 76052 250 6 Australia
ISBN 978 1 76052 750 1 UK

A catalogue record for this book is available from the British Library.

Printed by 1010 Printing International Limited, China